MY SCHOOL DAY FROM A TO Z

**R. G. Collins, Ed.D
And Liam Collins**

This book is dedicated to my sons, daughter-in-laws, and grandsons Ben, Liam, Aiden, Kyler, and Cameron. Thank you Liam for your ideas, inspiration, and support in helping me complete this book.

Aa	Bb	Cc	Dd	Ee	Ff
Gg	Hh	Ii	Jj	Kk	Ll
Mm	Nn	Oo	Pp	Qq	Rr
Ss	Tt	Uu	Vv	Ww	Xx
		Yy	Zz		

A is for alphabet I learn each day.

B is for bus I ride to school.

C is for cafeteria, where I eat breakfast and lunch.

D is for door to my classroom

E is for early arrival to school

F is for fun with my friends.

G is for glue I use on my artwork.

H is for hand I raise to ask questions.

I is for Iguana I see in the science classroom.

J is for jumping rope in gym class.

K is for keep your hands and feet to yourself.

L is for listen so you can learn from your teacher.

M is for media center,
where I read books.

N is for the nice people I see everywhere I go.

O is for outside fun on the playground

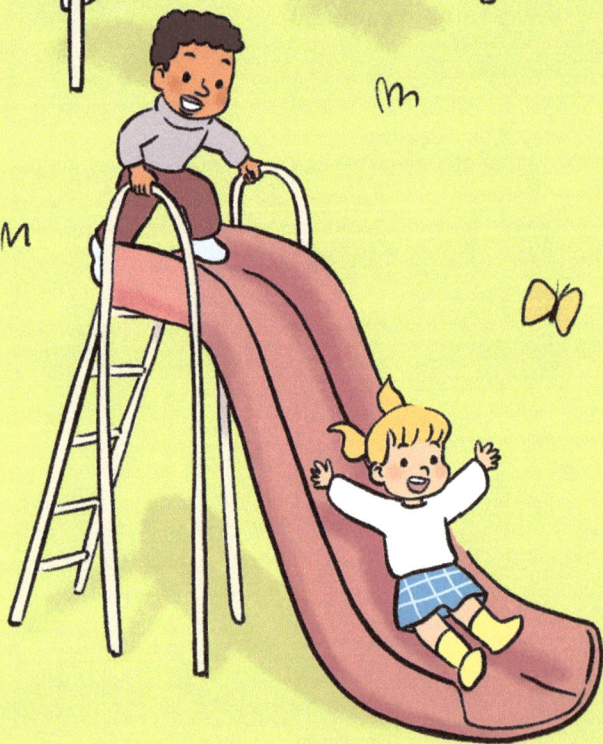

P is for pencil I use to write my name.

Q is for quiet please, so you can hear your teacher.

R is for ruler to measure my pencil.

S is for science project.

T is for telling time on the clock.

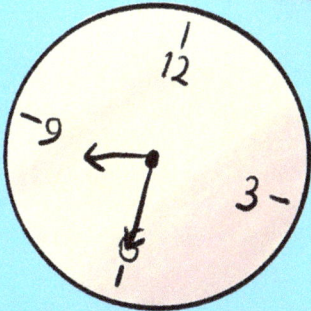

U is for uniforms everyone wears.

V is for vegetables I eat for lunch.

W is for walk in the hallway. Never run.

X is for xylophone I play during music class.

Y is for you are my best friend.

Z is for field trip to the Zoo.

www.ingramcontent.com/pod-product-compliance
Lightning Source LLC
Chambersburg PA
CBHW042108040426
42448CB00002B/187